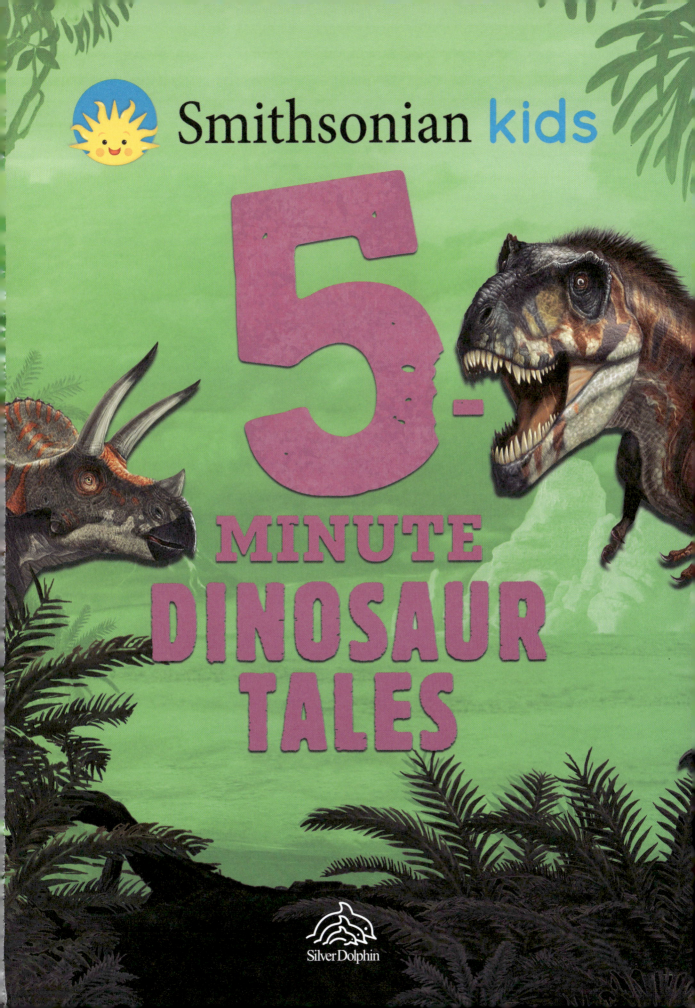

Silver Dolphin Books
An imprint of Printers Row Publishing Group
A division of Readerlink Distribution Services, LLC
9717 Pacific Heights Blvd, San Diego, CA 92121
www.silverdolphinbooks.com

Copyright © 2024 Printers Row Publishing Group and the Smithsonian
All rights reserved.
No part of this publication may be reproduced, distributed, or transmitted in any form or by any means, including photocopying, recording, or other electronic or mechanical methods, without the prior written permission of the publisher, except in the case of brief quotations embodied in critical reviews and certain other noncommercial uses permitted by copyright law.

Printers Row Publishing Group is a division of Readerlink Distribution Services, LLC.
Silver Dolphin Books is a registered trademark of Readerlink Distribution Services, LLC.
The name of the Smithsonian Institution and the sunburst logo are registered trademarks of the Smithsonian Institution. For more information, please visit www.si.edu
The Smithsonian is the world's largest museum and research complex, dedicated to public education, national service, and scholarship in the arts, Smithsonian sciences, and history.

All notations of errors or omissions should be addressed to Silver Dolphin Books, Editorial Department, at the above address.

Smithsonian Enterprises:
Avery Naughton, Licensing Coordinator
Paige Towler, Editorial Lead
Jill Corcoran, Senior Director, Licensed Publishing
Brigid Ferraro, Vice President of New Business and Licensing
Carol LeBlanc, President
National Museum of Natural History:
Matthew T. Miller, Museum Specialist

ISBN: 978-1-6672-0739-1
Manufactured, printed, and assembled in Heshan, China.
First printing, November 2024. LP/11/24
28 27 26 25 24   1 2 3 4 5

Image credits: James St. John, Jeremy Knight, Emőke Dénes, Susannah Maidment et al. & Natural History Museum, London, Chris Light, The Field Museum, Chicago, Axel Maurusza, Ghedoghedo, Jeffrey Beall, Michael Gray, James D. San Antonio1*, Mary H. Schweitzer2,3,4, Shane T. Jensen5, Raghu Kalluri6,7, Michael Buckley8,9, Joseph P. R. O. Orgel10*, Michelle Pemberton, Kenneth Carpenter, 3blindMies, Ghedoghedo, Nizar Ibrahim, Paul C. Sereno, David J. Varricchio, David M. Martill, Didier B. Dutheil, David M. Unwin, Lahssen Baidder, Hans C. E. Larsson, Samir Zouhri, Abdelhadi Kaoukaya, Mike Bowler, Bramfab, Susannah Maidment et al. & Natural History Museum, London, ケラトプスユウタ

Every effort has been made to contact copyright holders for the images in this book. If you are the copyright holder of any uncredited image herein, please contact us at Silver Dolphin Books, 9717 Pacific Heights Blvd, San Diego, CA 92121.

TABLE OF CONTENTS

Welcome to the World, Baby *Maiasaura*! 5

A Closer Look: *Stegosaurus* 21

Pachycephalosaurus* versus *Pachycephalosaurus .. 37

A Closer Look: *Brachiosaurus* 53

King of the Dinosaurs: *Tyrannosaurus rex* ... 69

A Closer Look: *Tyrannosaurus rex* 85

***Centrosaurus* Stampede** **101**

A Closer Look: *Ankylosaurus* **115**

Prehistoric Animals in the Air and in the Sea **131**

A Closer Look: *Triceratops* **147**

Velociraptor* versus *Protoceratops **163**

A Closer Look: *Spinosaurus* **179**

Welcome to the World, Baby *Maiasaura*!

By Courtney Acampora

Crunch, crunch. A baby *Maiasaura* (my-ah-SORE-ah) emerges from her egg. This hadrosaur, a duck-billed plant-eating dinosaur, lives during the Cretaceous period, 76 million years ago in what will one day be known as Montana. As the baby *Maiasaura* breaks out of her egg, she realizes that she isn't alone.

All around her are hundreds of nests full of babies and eggs. *Maiasaura* are social creatures that nest in groups of up to a thousand. There are other babies that are new to the world like her, and others are still inside their eggs.

Baby *Maiasaura* is now ready to explore—and for now her nest will do! She is covered in rotting vegetation that keeps her nice and warm. She is enjoying the warmth and protection of her nest as she continues to grow and develop. Soon, she will be big enough to leave her nest.

The baby's mother built her nest out of mud and vegetation. She shaped the nest into a crater and laid her eggs in the center. And this baby *Maiasaura* is not alone in the nest! Baby *Maiasaura* is huddled in the nest with her siblings. Each year, the mother *Maiasaura* lays up to forty eggs. Baby *Maiasaura*'s siblings haven't broken out of their eggs just yet.

Maiasaura live in herds made up of males and females. If one mother leaves to search for food, the other *Maiasaura* keep an eye on all the nests. Their name even means "good mother lizard" because they nurture their young.

This baby *Maiasaura* depends on her mother to bring food back to the nest. She's much too young and weak to leave her nest and fend for herself. So, her mother leaves the nesting ground and searches for her favorite plants to bring back to feed her baby. The plants help the baby *Maiasaura* grow big and strong.

The baby's mother is a medium-sized dinosaur that is 20 feet long and weighs around 8,000 pounds. For now, the baby *Maiasaura* weighs just a couple pounds and is 12 inches in length. Her body is skinny with a small head and large eyes. Eventually, by age eight, she will grow to her full size.

Who is this? It's a young *Maiasaura* from another nest! He has emerged from his nest and is now exploring his neighbors' nest. Nearby, his mother's snort means it's time to leave and look for food. The baby *Maiasaura* peeks over the nest's side and watches the young *Maiasaura* and his mother trot off into the forest.

Though the warm nest is a nice place to stay, it's getting crowded! When the baby *Maiasaura* broke out of her shell, she realized there were other eggs in the nest. And now some of her siblings have hatched as well!

Screech, screech. Her siblings are a noisy bunch. The good news is that in a few weeks, baby *Maiasaura* will be big enough to leave the nest and explore her habitat.

But until then, the baby *Maiasaura* is on the lookout. In the distance, she sees a large lake sparkling in the sunshine. Up above, a pterosaur soars over the nesting ground. And nearby, other *Maiasaura* mothers guard their nests and feed their young.

Maiasaura have strong eyesight and hearing to help protect them and their young from danger. A meat eater called *Stenonychosaurus* (sten-ON-ee-koh-SORE-us) likes to hide out in the plants surrounding the nesting site. The helpless baby dinosaurs and eggs are the perfect, easy snack. As long as the mothers are alert and on guard, the babies will be safe.

A couple of weeks later, baby *Maiasaura* is no longer a baby! At least in size. She's now big enough to leave the nest and join her mother beyond the nesting ground. But baby *Maiasaura*'s legs are a lot shorter than her mother's, so she needs to run to keep up!

Mother *Maiasaura* shows the baby where her favorite food grows. Instead of her mother bringing food to the nest, baby *Maiasaura* can now feed herself by selecting yummy leaves to eat. Her duck-billed beak is perfect for snipping leaves off branches.

As baby *Maiasaura* continues to grow and eventually matures into an adult, she will make her home in a herd of up to a thousand *Maiasaura*. The more eyes and ears in a herd, the safer the *Maiasaura* will be from hungry predators.

The herd will migrate to new feeding grounds where they will also lay their eggs and raise their young. This baby will one day have her own hatchlings and will care for them like her mother cared for her.

A CLOSER LOOK: *STEGOSAURUS*

By Courtney Acampora

STRIKING *STEGOSAURUS*

During the Late Jurassic period, 145 million years ago, *Stegosaurus* (STEG-oh-SORE-us) roamed its habitat in what is today Wyoming, Colorado, and Utah. This slow-moving plant eater browsed for plants to eat, and at the same time, it needed to be on constant guard from predators. Predators such as *Allosaurus* (AL-oh-SORE-us) were also on the lookout for animals like *Stegosaurus*—but for a meal.

Like other dinosaurs, *Stegosaurus* had a way to protect itself from hungry predators: its spiked tail. *Stegosaurus* could swing its powerful tail and strike a predator. *BAM!*

STEGOSAURUS UP CLOSE

STATS
PRONUNCIATION: **STEG-oh-SORE-us**
NAME MEANING: **Roofed Lizard**
SIZE: **30 feet long; 6,000 pounds**
WHEN IT LIVED: **Late Jurassic**
FOSSILS FOUND: **North America**

Compared to its body size, *Stegosaurus* had one of the smallest brains of any dinosaur.

Thick, scaly skin protected *Stegosaurus*'s neck.

Shorter front legs caused *Stegosaurus*'s head to be low to the ground, perfect for munching on plants!

SPIKES AND PLATES

Stegosaurus was as big as two rhinoceroses. It would have been a prime target for the hungry meat eaters of its day. *Stegosaurus*'s most recognizable feature was the seventeen bony plates that stood up along its back. The plates stood up to 2 feet tall and may have been used for protection, mating, defense, or temperature control.

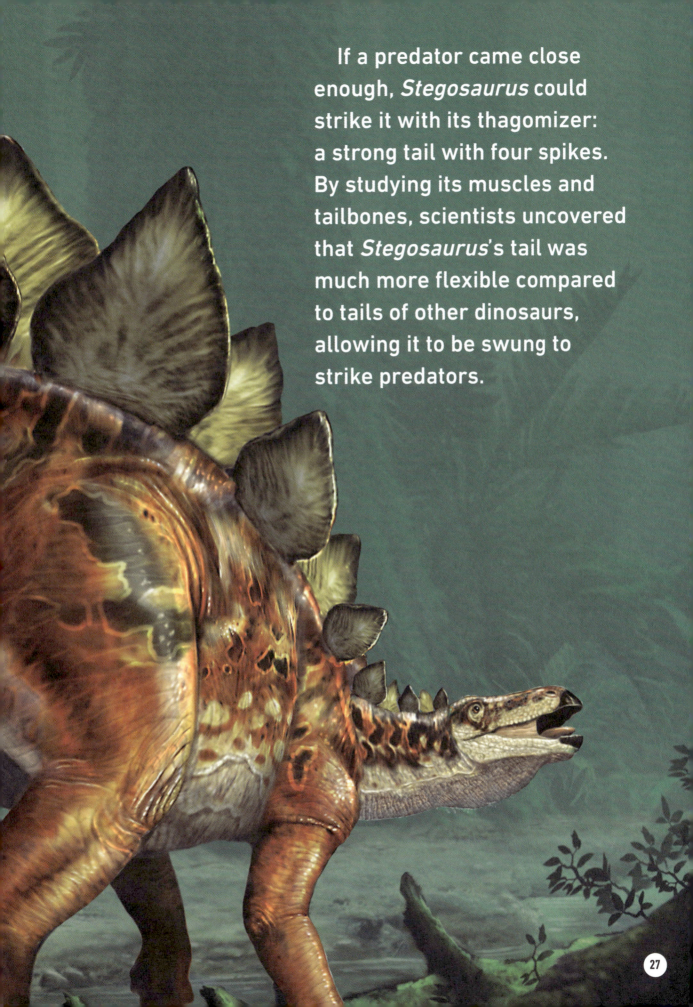

If a predator came close enough, *Stegosaurus* could strike it with its thagomizer: a strong tail with four spikes. By studying its muscles and tailbones, scientists uncovered that *Stegosaurus*'s tail was much more flexible compared to tails of other dinosaurs, allowing it to be swung to strike predators.

ON THE HUNT

Which dinosaurs did *Stegosaurus* need to look out for? Its two main predators were *Allosaurus* and *Ceratosaurus* (se-RAT-oh-SORE-us). *Allosaurus* was the apex predator of its habitat. This meat-eating dinosaur was 30 feet long and its mouth was full of serrated teeth, perfect for slicing into prey. One *Allosaurus* fossil was discovered with a circular hole in its pelvis—a hole created by a *Stegosaurus*'s barbed tail during a fight. Ouch!

Ceratosaurus was a meat-eating dinosaur that hunted and stalked prey like *Stegosaurus*. But at 30 feet long and 6,000 pounds, *Stegosaurus* was not small prey to catch. If *Ceratosaurus* was lucky and could defeat a *Stegosaurus*, it could do so with its fearsome jaws full of razor-sharp teeth.

WHERE DID *STEGOSAURUS* LIVE?

How do paleontologists learn about dinosaurs that roamed the earth millions of years ago? Fossils. The Morrison Formation is a series of rocks in Utah and Colorado from the Jurassic period. It is one of the most fossil-rich places on Earth.

The Morrison Formation

The fossilized plants found in the Morrison Formation offer a sneak peek into what *Stegosaurus*'s habitat was like. It was likely a shrubland with forest and was much warmer and humid than today. By studying the Morrison Formation fossils, scientists gather clues about *Stegosaurus* and its habitat.

STEGOSAURUS DISCOVERY

In 1877, a fossil hunter named Arthur Lakes uncovered a dinosaur fossil in Morrison, Colorado. He shared the fossil with paleontologist Othniel Charles Marsh, who named the dinosaur *Stegosaurus,* or "roofed lizard," because of the mysterious fossilized plates that he believed covered the dinosaur like roof shingles.

Othniel Charles Marsh

At first, Marsh thought the creature was a swimming reptile with flat plates like those on a turtle's shell. In 1891, Marsh changed his mind and theorized that *Stegosaurus*'s signature plates stood upright on its back. Throughout his life, Marsh named many other dinosaurs, such as *Triceratops* (tri-SER-ah-tops), *Allosaurus*, and *Diplodocus* (DIP-low-DOCK-us).

SOPHIE THE *STEGOSAURUS*

In 2003, at Red Canyon Ranch in Wyoming, paleontologist Bob Simon discovered a *Stegosaurus* fossil. After three weeks of excavation, the 150-million-year-old fossil was removed from the earth.

Red Canyon Ranch, Wyoming

Though scientists are unsure if the dinosaur was male or female, the fossil is named Sophie and it's the most complete *Stegosaurus* fossil discovered so far. At the time Sophie died, it was a young adult about the size of a rhinoceros and weighing about 3,500 pounds. Sophie's fossilized body is made up of 300 bones, with only the base of its tail and left foreleg missing. Today, Sophie is on display at London's Natural History Museum.

Sophie the *Stegosaurus*

SPIKY *STEGOSAURUS*

Because of fossils like Sophie, scientists are continually discovering more information about this fascinating Jurassic plant eater. With plates along its back and a spiky tail, *Stegosaurus* is one of the most recognizable dinosaur species.

Pachycephalosaurus versus Pachycephalosaurus

By Maggie Fischer

The air feels humid in the misty forest as the morning sun creeps slowly into the sky. The soft hum of hidden insects is interrupted by the sound of *Quetzalcoatlus* (KWET-zal-koh-AT-lus) flapping overhead.

Quetzalcoatlus's 40-foot wingspan darkens the muddy ground as it passes the rising sun. *Pachycephalosaurus* (pa-kee-seh-fuh-luh-SAW-ruhz) wakes, listening carefully, on alert.

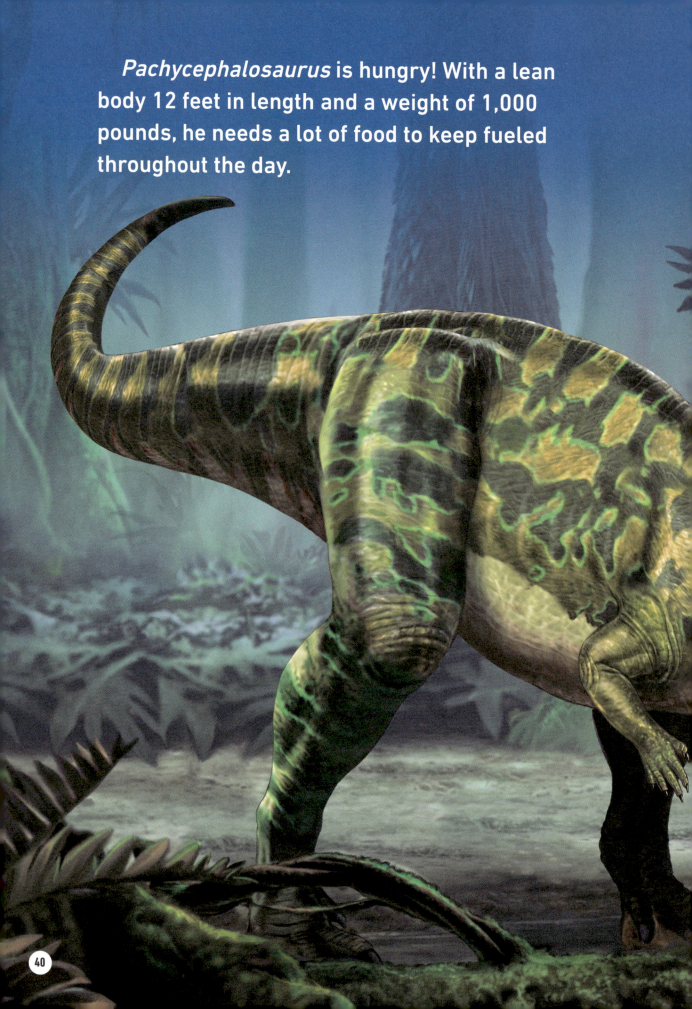

Pachycephalosaurus is hungry! With a lean body 12 feet in length and a weight of 1,000 pounds, he needs a lot of food to keep fueled throughout the day.

Carefully, he walks farther into the forest, grazing on nearby ferns and grasses. He uses his pointed beak to quickly tear off leaves from bushes and low trees and scours the ground for crunchy bugs and seeds, grinding them between the teeth in his beak.

A rustle in the grass interrupts *Pachycephalosaurus*'s breakfast. He looks around, tense. Could it be a ferocious predator watching him and ready to strike?

42

The fierce *Tyrannosaurus rex* (tie-RAN-oh-SORE-us rex) hunts in these forests, and a smaller omnivore like *Pachycephalosaurus* would be tempting prey for this large predator. *Rustle, rustle.* The sound is coming closer.

Pachycephalosaurus has a split second to decide—run or face possible danger? He decides to stay put. Luckily, he has a defense mechanism that comes in handy.

Armed with a dome-like head covered in short, spiky horns, *Pachycephalosaurus* is no defenseless target. His 9-inch-thick skull can be used like a battering ram against enemies. His skull is twenty times thicker than that of other dinosaurs. Lowering his head slightly in anticipation of an attack, *Pachycephalosaurus* waits.

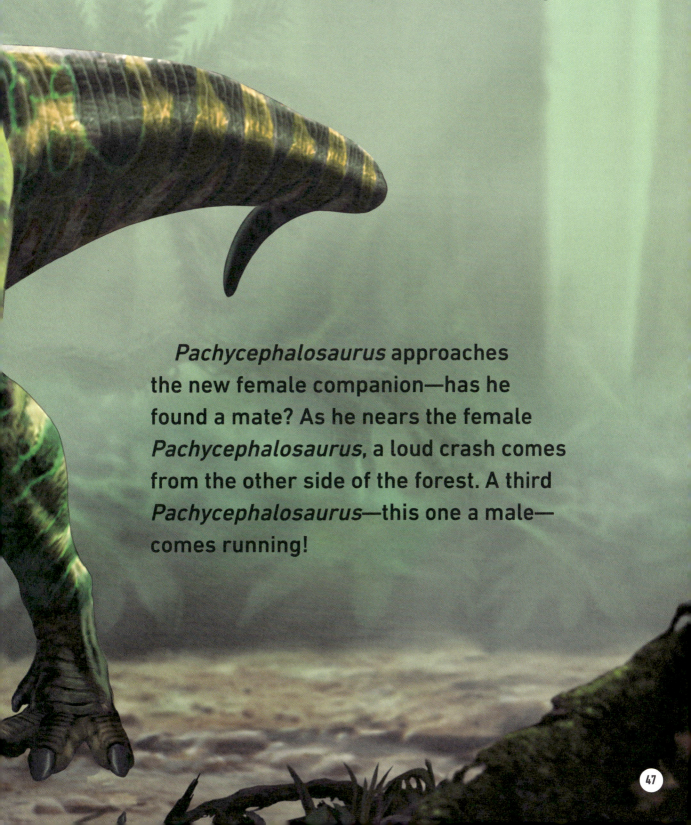

Instead of a roaring *Tyrannosaurus rex*, a female *Pachycephalosaurus* stomps out of the brush. Her domed head bumps against the branches as she enters the clearing.

Pachycephalosaurus approaches the new female companion—has he found a mate? As he nears the female *Pachycephalosaurus*, a loud crash comes from the other side of the forest. A third *Pachycephalosaurus*—this one a male—comes running!

The first *Pachycephalosaurus* quickly moves to battle for his potential mate. He will prove to her that he is the stronger dinosaur of the two. Using his thick, strong legs, he pushes off and races toward his foe.

He juts out his thick skull just in time—*CRACK!* Both *Pachycephalosaurus'* thick skulls absorb the blow. The two *Pachycephalosaurus* males butt heads, the sound of their spiky domes colliding echoes through the forest.

Again and again, the male *Pachycephalosaurus* crash into each other, head-to-head or in the flank, tail, or chest. Their bodies are covered in thick, scaly skin that also protects them from injuries.

Finally, the first *Pachycephalosaurus* lands a crushing blow to his opponent's side, knocking him over. The competing male concedes defeat and slowly stomps back into the forest. The female is impressed by the winner's fighting skills. She decides to stay.

Now *Pachycephalosaurus* and his mate search the surrounding area for food. Together, they search the forest for tasty leaves and seeds to fill their bellies. Soon, they will have eggs to nurture, and will need to forage for their babies too. Eventually, they will usher in more *Pachycephalosaurus*—with their father's skull-cracking skills.

A CLOSER LOOK: *BRACHIOSAURUS*

By Maggie Fischer

TOWERING BRACHIOSAURUS

One of the largest dinosaurs to roam the earth, *Brachiosaurus* (BRAK-ee-oh-SORE-us) was a sight to behold. Weighing over 150,000 pounds and towering twice as tall as a giraffe, *Brachiosaurus* needed a lot of food to survive. This massive herbivore ate up to 400 pounds of plants each day, usually without needing to move around much. Its long neck allowed it to reach into the tallest trees and forage in the forest canopy.

Because of its size, *Brachiosaurus* was slow-moving, but that same stature helped to protect it against predators who found it difficult to take down such a gigantic creature.

BRACHIOSAURUS UP CLOSE

Relatively small compared to its body, *Brachiosaurus*'s skull was lightweight so that its long neck could support it.

Brachiosaurus did not chew its food. Its jaw collected food and the tongue pushed it down.

Brachiosaurus's long neck allowed it to browse without needing to move around much in search of food.

Longer front legs helped *Brachiosaurus* reach the tallest trees for a leafy snack.

STATS
PRONUNCIATION: **BRAK-ee-oh-SORE-us**
NAME MEANING: **Arm Lizard**
SIZE: **85 feet long; 150,000 pounds**
WHEN IT LIVED: **Late Jurassic**
FOSSILS FOUND: **North America, Africa, Europe**

Paleontologists theorize that *Brachiosaurus*'s size was due to its diet. Plants were difficult to digest and may have required an extra-large digestive tract.

DINO OUT OF WATER

Because of its size, experts once believed that *Brachiosaurus* must have lived in the water; a hypothesis we now know is wrong. It was supposed that a water habitat would keep its body buoyant and ease the pressure of its weight—as much as four African elephants! It was once thought that *Brachiosaurus* also had nostril holes located on the top of its skull, suggesting a snorkel-like use for its nose that would come in handy living in the water.

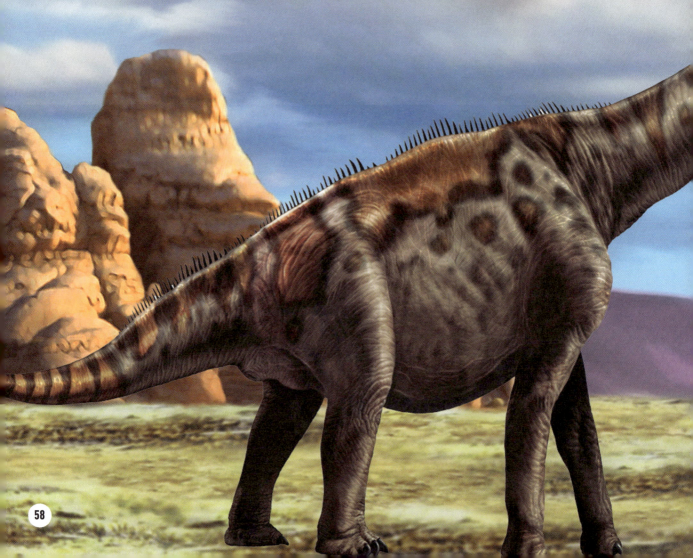

However, further study revealed that the pressure of water deep enough to submerge the *Brachiosaurus* would have crushed its lungs, making it impossible to breathe in air. Their sturdy skeletons were found to be strong enough to carry their weight on land. Other studies have shown that *Brachiosaurus* nostrils were located at the front of the snout, just like on other animals.

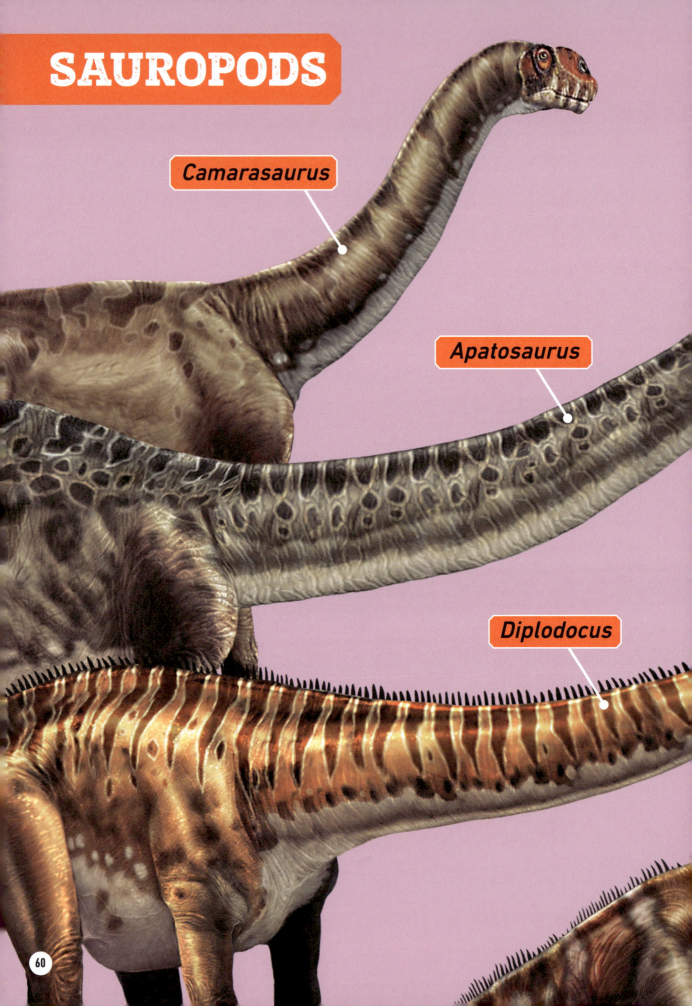

Brachiosaurus was part of a group of dinosaurs called sauropods, identifiable by their long necks and small heads. With teeth that were spoon-shaped, sauropods likely swallowed stones that would grind up the massive amounts of plant matter they ate.

All sauropods were large, and their giant hip bones supported their trunk-like legs, wide bodies, and long tails. *Brachiosaurus* was one of the biggest sauropods, but the smallest sauropods were still a whopping 50 feet in length.

Brachiosaurus

A GIANT DISCOVERY

Brachiosaurus fossils were first found in North America in what is now Colorado. This location, part of the Morrison Formation, is home to many fossil discoveries from the Late Jurassic period.

In 1903, paleontologist Elmer Riggs discovered several fossils that had such unusual proportions he believed they belonged to an undiscovered dinosaur. The humerus was huge, leading to the image we have of the *Brachiosaurus*, the "arm lizard," with staggering height. The bones were bigger than any known dinosaurs at the time, so Riggs named the new dinosaur *Brachiosaurus altithorax* to distinguish it from the *Diplodocus* and *Apatosaurus*, previously found in the same area.

TANZANIAN TWIN

Brachiosaurus fossils found in Tanzania looked like those found by Elmer Riggs. The fossils found in Africa were more complete and allowed paleontologists to develop a clearer picture of the mysterious giant that was *Brachiosaurus*.

Tanzania

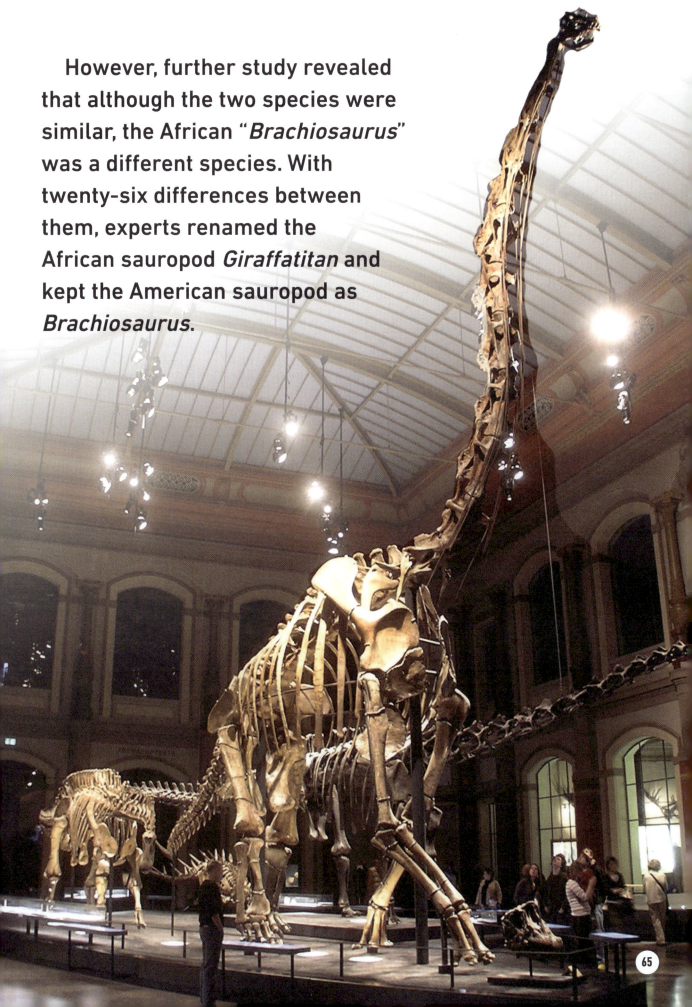

However, further study revealed that although the two species were similar, the African "*Brachiosaurus*" was a different species. With twenty-six differences between them, experts renamed the African sauropod *Giraffatitan* and kept the American sauropod as *Brachiosaurus*.

BABY *BRACHIOSAURUS*

In 2007, a juvenile sauropod skeleton was found in Wyoming's Howe-Stephens Quarry. Originally thought to be a *Diplodocus*, preparation of the partial skeleton revealed more similarities to *Brachiosaurus* instead.

Baby sauropod skeleton

Wyoming's Howe-Stephens Quarry

Scientists are waiting to classify the dinosaur skeleton until more information can be obtained. Because dinosaurs changed a lot as they grew from babies to adults, a juvenile dinosaur skeleton can only tell experts so much about what the adult dinosaur looked like.

MISTAKEN IDENTITY

Although there's much more to learn about *Brachiosaurus*, many things can be deciphered about how it lived based on where its fossils were found. With every mistaken identification, paleontologists get one step closer to the truth. One day we'll know even more about the massive *Brachiosaurus*.

King of the Dinosaurs: *Tyrannosaurus rex*

By Courtney Acampora

In a forested river valley buzzing with insects and dappled with lush plants, a giant's footsteps rattle the ground.

The giant scans the landscape, searching for its prey. Any prey will do, and almost all of them won't stand a chance against this giant predator.

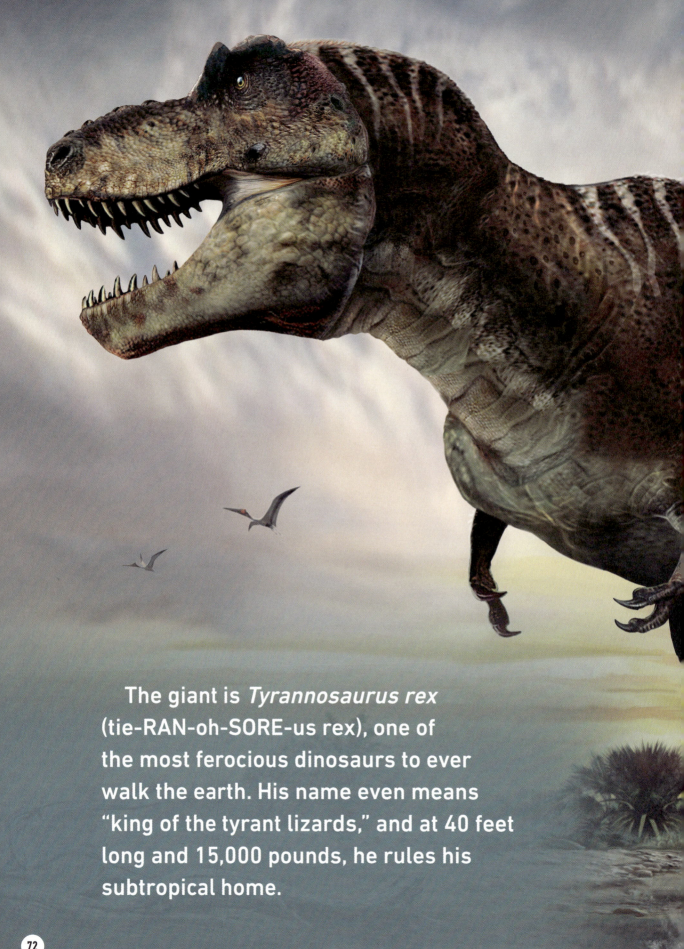

The giant is *Tyrannosaurus rex* (tie-RAN-oh-SORE-us rex), one of the most ferocious dinosaurs to ever walk the earth. His name even means "king of the tyrant lizards," and at 40 feet long and 15,000 pounds, he rules his subtropical home.

T. rex's mouth is full of serrated teeth that are each the size of a banana and made to puncture flesh. Using his strong 4-foot-long jaws, he can eat 100 pounds of meat in just one bite. He's built for the hunt. He can run 12 miles per hour using his long, thick tail to help him balance as he runs.

In addition to his size, strength, and teeth, *T. rex* also has an incredible sense of smell, which means no prey is safe. *T. rex*'s nose will lead him straight to his meal. Today, his nose is leading him to the swamp.

T. rex enters the sun-dappled swamp, making his way through the trees draped with moss and buzzing with dragonflies. He trudges through the shallow water, walking further in the swamp. The smell is getting stronger.

Up ahead, he spots a herd of *Triceratops* (tri-SER-ah-tops) in a clearing. The herd has stopped for a drink of water. *Snap, crunch.* The *Triceratops* hear movement nearby. One of the *Triceratops* turns his head, but it's too late. *T. rex* has spotted the herd and now he's running through the swamp toward the plant eaters.

Armed with three sharp horns on their heads, the horns are *Triceratops*' only defense against *T. rex*. The *Triceratops* race as fast as they can through the swampy water. A baby *Triceratops* almost falls to the *T. rex*, but a quick turn around a tree saves him.

This herd of *Triceratops* is a strong group, and their knowledge and navigation of the swamp helps them escape *T. rex*. *T. rex*'s big feet have sunk into thick, sludgy mud, allowing the *Triceratops* to escape. This *T. rex* prefers sick and injured *Triceratops,* which are much easier to catch.

T. rex will have to find his meal elsewhere. He makes his way out of the swamp and into the valley clearing. He hears scurrying through the trees. He finds a new scent to follow.

In the clearing next to a fallen tree, *T. rex* spots the carcass of a young *Triceratops*. *T. rex* is a powerful predator, but he's also a scavenger and will feast on a dead dinosaur if it's available. This *Triceratops* was an easy find.

T. rex dines on the carcass, but it isn't long before his neighbors smell the meal and emerge from the forest. Another *T. rex* also comes forward. The first *T. rex* needs to either eat very quickly or defend his find from the other scavengers.

Dakotaraptor (da-KO-tah-RAP-tor) are also mighty predators in this habitat, and *T. rex*'s competition. Though not as large as *T. rex*, *Dakotaraptor* could easily take down a baby *T. rex*, using its sharp teeth. Today, a group of *Dakotaraptor* are also interested in the meal.

ROOOOOOAAR! *T. rex* lets the other dinosaurs know that this carcass is his. The *Dakotaraptor* could use their sharp teeth and claws to try to attack the *T. rex*, but this *T. rex* is much too big. The *Dakotaraptor* decide to move on. They'll have better luck finding another carcass that *T. rex* hasn't gotten to yet. The two *T. rex* go head-to-head, and the second *T. rex* is victorious. After receiving a mighty bite to his face, the first *T. rex* leaves defeated.

T. rex is hungry and needs a meal to keep his energy up. In the distance, Ankylosaurus (ang-KEE-loh-SORE-us), an armored plant eater, spots the T. rex. At all times, Ankylosaurus is on the lookout for T. rex.

T. rex scans the landscape looking for his next meal. As one of the largest predators to walk the earth, the other dinosaur species he meets are always on guard. If he comes near them, they won't stand a chance. He's a determined predator who rules this habitat.

A CLOSER LOOK: TYRANNOSAURUS REX

By Maggie Fischer

KING OF THE TYRANT LIZARDS

The terrifying *Tyrannosaurus rex* (tie-RAN-oh-SORE-us rex), or "king of the tyrant lizards," ruled western North America during the Cretaceous period. A ferocious meat eater, *T. rex* used its keen sense of smell, razor-sharp claws, and giant teeth to capture and tear into prey.

With a heavy body the size of a school bus, and a thirst for prey, *T. rex* was a formidable predator, even to large herbivores like *Triceratops* (tri-SER-ah-tops) and *Edmontosaurus* (ed-MON-toe-SORE-us). The sounds of its feet stomping across the plain meant danger for nearby prey.

T. REX UP CLOSE

STATS
PRONUNCIATION: tie-RAN-oh-SORE-us rex
NAME MEANING: Tyrant Lizard King
SIZE: 40 feet long; 15,000 pounds
WHEN IT LIVED: Cretaceous
FOSSILS FOUND: Western United States and Canada

A long, thick tail balanced *T. rex*'s enormous body and helped it move quickly.

Due to its weight, *T. rex* could probably walk up to only 12 miles per hour on its thick legs.

T. rex had forward-facing eyes, which helped it track prey it was chasing. Forward-facing eyes are common features in predators.

T. rex had an amazing sense of smell. It used the olfactory portion of its brain to process smells better than any living animal today.

With sixty serrated teeth, each 12 inches long, it was easy for *T. rex* to tear into the tough skin of its prey.

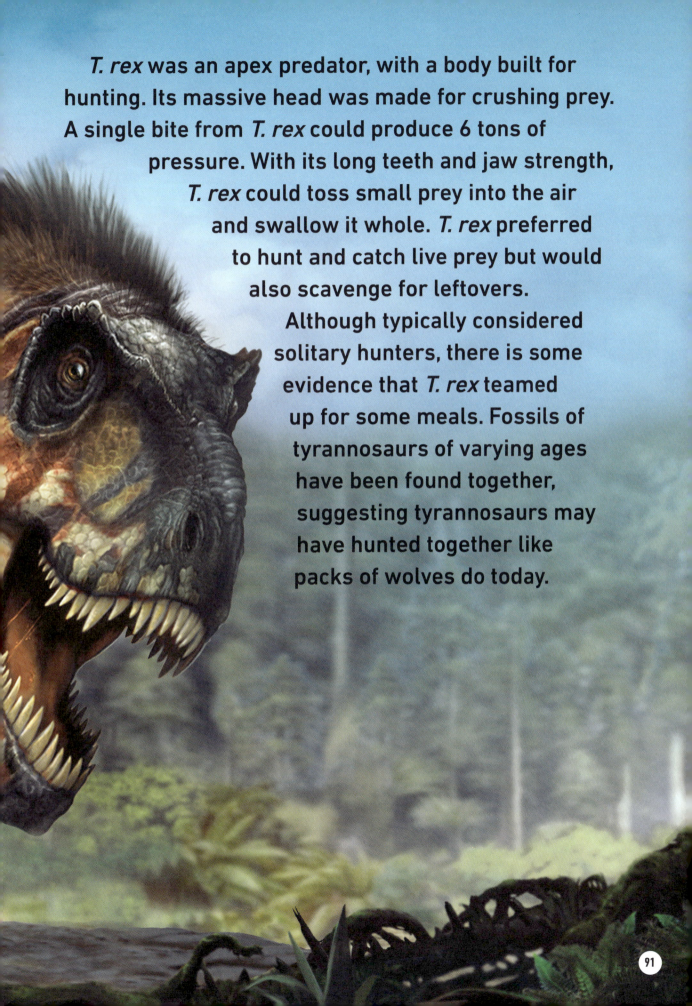

T. rex was an apex predator, with a body built for hunting. Its massive head was made for crushing prey. A single bite from T. rex could produce 6 tons of pressure. With its long teeth and jaw strength, T. rex could toss small prey into the air and swallow it whole. T. rex preferred to hunt and catch live prey but would also scavenge for leftovers.

Although typically considered solitary hunters, there is some evidence that T. rex teamed up for some meals. Fossils of tyrannosaurs of varying ages have been found together, suggesting tyrannosaurs may have hunted together like packs of wolves do today.

SOFT SPOTS

Despite its effectiveness as a top predator, T. rex had some unusual attributes. Its arms were short and stubby, a mystery to experts. Some think they were an unnecessary feature left over from evolutionary changes. Others think that the short arms helped hold prey down while T. rex's mighty jaws bit into vital areas.

Faster dinosaurs had an advantage against the lumbering T. rex—its heavy legs couldn't move faster than a brisk walk. Any speedier, and scientists believe the weight of the T. rex would shatter its leg bones. Quicker dinosaurs could outrun the apex predator, but T. rex could walk long distances to eventually catch their meal.

THEROPODS

T. rex

Allosaurus

T. rex was a theropod, meaning "beast-footed." Mostly made up of meat eaters that walked on two legs like the ferocious *T. rex*, theropods were characterized by hollow bones, backward-curved teeth, and large eyes.

Other prehistoric theropods include *Velociraptor* (vel-OSS-ee-RAP-tor), *Allosaurus* (AL-oh-SORE-us), *Utahraptor* (YOU-tah-RAP-tor), and more. Theropods are the only dinosaurs that still exist—they're alive in the form of birds! Birds have the distinct features of theropods (including their hollow bones needed for flight). Recent discoveries even suggest that *T. rex* may have been partially covered in feathers.

SUE THE *T. REX*

In 1990, one of the most famous dinosaur fossils was discovered on the Cheyenne River Sioux Tribe Reservation in South Dakota. The *T. rex* fossil was discovered by (and named after) paleontologist Sue Hendrickson. It took a crew of six people seventeen days to unearth the giant *T. rex*.

Cheyenne River Sioux Tribe Reservation

Although scientists are unsure if it was a female or male, Sue is the largest, best-preserved *T. rex* fossil ever found. The dinosaur is 42 feet long and 13 feet tall at the hip. Sue helped scientists learn a lot about the amazing *T. rex*, including its lifespan—Sue was 28 years old when it died!

MORE DINO DISCOVERIES

T. rex has been part of multiple amazing discoveries in paleontology. In 2007, paleontologist Mary Schweitzer made a groundbreaking discovery: soft tissue in the form of proteins in a T. rex fossil. Previously, no one imagined that proteins could have possibly survived millions of years.

T. rex tooth

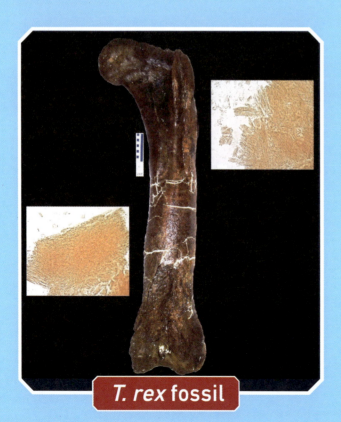

T. rex fossil

Coprolite, or fossilized dung, is another way that scientists learn more about prehistoric life. One of the largest coprolites ever found was larger than a loaf of bread—and was believed to have been produced by a *T. rex*.

Coprolite

TERRIFIC *T. REX*

New information may adjust how we see these predatorial powerhouses, but one thing is for certain: *T. rex* was a force to be reckoned with in the Cretaceous period. Whether it hunted in herds or kept to itself, it was always searching for its next meal. Using its uncanny sense of smell to sniff out hiding herbivores, *T. rex* didn't need speed—its mighty jaws could finish a fight with a decisive *CRUNCH!*

Centrosaurus Stampede

By Devra Newberger Speregen

It's early morning and baby *Centrosaurus* (cen-troh-SORE-us) wakes up hungry. He stretches his short little legs and follows his family to the river to look for food. This herbivore, a plant-eating dinosaur, lives in the Cretaceous period in what will someday become Alberta, Canada. The warm climate makes it the perfect place to call home. The temperature is just right for lots of plants and flowers to grow.

Baby *Centrosaurus* and his family do not go alone to the river. They travel with a herd, or group, of thousands of *Centrosaurus* families. Baby *Centrosaurus* loves to race ahead to walk with other babies, but he never roams too far from his family.

Along the way, baby *Centrosaurus* looks for low-lying shrubs to munch on because that's all he can reach. *Centrosaurus* are medium-sized dinosaurs with short legs and heads that are close to the ground. They also have short, inflexible necks, so they can't reach food that is too high up.

Baby *Centrosaurus* looks a lot like a modern-day rhinoceros, with a pointy horn on the front of his nose. Since baby *Centrosaurus* is still young, his horn is very small and isn't curved yet. As he gets older, it will start to curve forward.

When the herd reaches the riverbank, it feasts on yummy fern leaves and flowering plants. Some of the leaves are very thick and hard to chew. It's a good thing baby *Centrosaurus* has a beak like a parrot and strong jaw muscles. And his sharp upper and lower teeth work like scissors when he chews, so he can slice through the tough plants.

Baby *Centrosaurus* has between 112 and 124 teeth. They are packed closely together, and they help him cut and grind through tough, thick leaves and bark. Plus, all *Centrosaurus* have up to five brand-new teeth under each tooth, waiting to break through after their regular teeth get worn down. In the distance, lightning strikes and the herd keeps moving.

Having filled his belly, baby *Centrosaurus* swims and plays in the river with the other babies. They play in the mudflats too. While they play, the *Centrosaurus* fathers stand in a circle around the babies to protect them from hungry predators. They face outward, always on the lookout for danger.

The *Centrosaurus* fathers hear a loud rumble. It could be a menacing *Gorgosaurus* (GOR-goh-sore-us) approaching. Or it could be the sound of thunder and the storm coming. They grow anxious and warn their families that something is not right.

Grown-up *Centrosaurus* measure about 20 feet long and weigh around 5,000 pounds. They are enormous! But they are no match for *Gorgosaurus,* who is 26 feet long and has a mouth full of razor-sharp teeth made to tear into prey.

Centrosaurus has big, sharp horns that can be used to scare off attackers. But do they stand a chance against a predator like *Gorgosaurus*? At the first sign of danger at the river, the *Centrosaurus* fathers know they must act fast to get their families to safety.

Baby *Centrosaurus* hears his father's warning. He stops playing. He knows he must stay close to his family and starts to run. With four very strong but little legs, baby *Centrosaurus* runs as fast as he can!

The herd sticks together and runs in the same direction toward safety. They run toward what will become their new home: a place far away from the river, far away from *Gorgosaurus*, and far away from the threat of flash floods and storms. The ground rumbles beneath them as they run. And the noise from tens of thousands of *Centrosaurus* running at the same time is deafening. It's a *Centrosaurus* stampede!

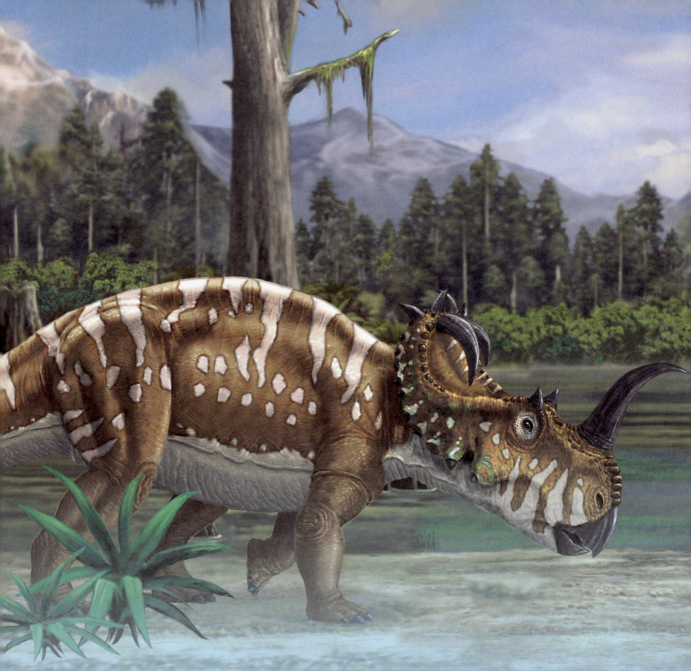

Luckily, baby *Centrosaurus* and his family make it to safety. Many of the other *Centrosaurus* families do too. Unfortunately, some *Centrosaurus* do not make it out of the path of the ferocious dinosaur. Dinosaur tracks, fossils, and bones from the *Centrosaurus* stampede will be discovered millions of years later. They will tell the story of baby *Centrosaurus* and all the *Centrosaurus* who lived, traveled, grazed, and stampeded together.

A CLOSER LOOK: ANKYLOSAURUS

By Dienesa Le

MEET ANKYLOSAURUS

During the Cretaceous period, dinosaurs lived on every continent on Earth and evolved into a wide variety of species. In what is now northern United States and southern Canada, one dinosaur was built like a tank, covered in protective armor. Plates with spikes and horns coated its back similar to a crocodile or armadillo. This dinosaur was called *Ankylosaurus* (ang-KEE-loh-SORE-us).

Ankylosaurus belonged to a group of dinosaurs called ornithischians, or bird-hipped dinosaurs. This group was very diverse, but all of them were herbivores—dinosaurs that only ate plants.

ANKYLOSAURUS UP CLOSE

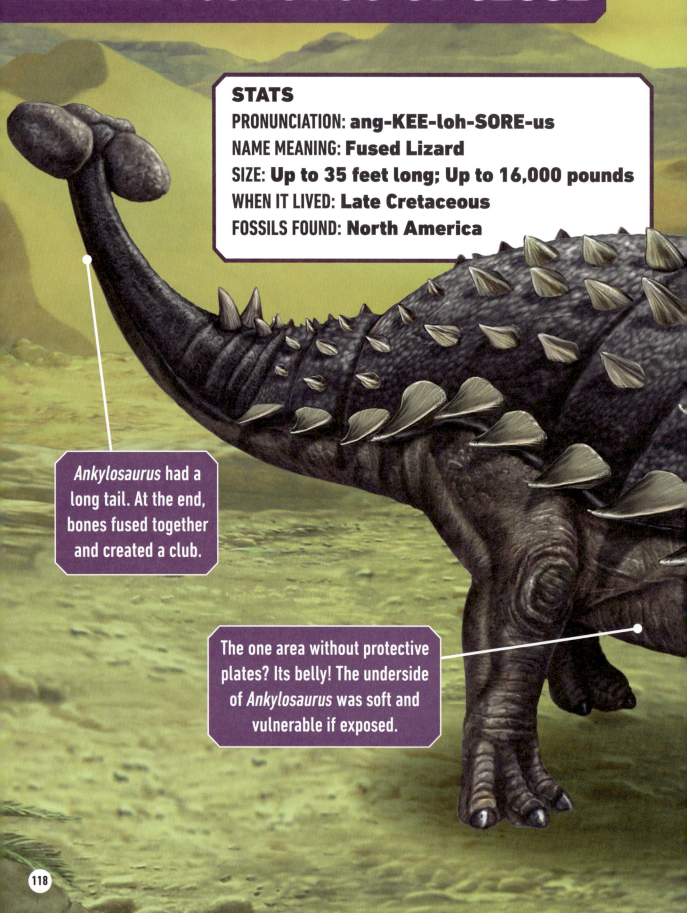

STATS
PRONUNCIATION: ang-KEE-loh-SORE-us
NAME MEANING: Fused Lizard
SIZE: Up to 35 feet long; Up to 16,000 pounds
WHEN IT LIVED: Late Cretaceous
FOSSILS FOUND: North America

Ankylosaurus had a long tail. At the end, bones fused together and created a club.

The one area without protective plates? Its belly! The underside of *Ankylosaurus* was soft and vulnerable if exposed.

SUITED FOR PROTECTION

Ankylosaurus was as big as an African elephant and as slow as one too. Its stout, bulky body and short legs meant it moved at a slower pace, making it an easy target for meat eaters. It was a dangerous time when predators, like *T. rex*, were giant!

But *Ankylosaurus* had plenty of protection—an impressive armor of plates, spikes, and horns. It stayed low and flat to the ground to protect its belly. A predator could try to attack the dinosaur's most vulnerable area. But since *Ankylosaurus* was already low to the ground and heavy, it would be tough to tip over!

FRIENDS IN ARMOR

Ankylosaurus was an armored dinosaur just like *Stegosaurus* (STEG-oh-SORE-us), though they lived nearly 70 million years apart. Both dinosaurs had plates along their backs. While the plates on *Stegosaurus* stood upright, the protective plates on *Ankylosaurus* lay flat. This heavy-duty armor extended to the sides, neck, and head of *Ankylosaurus*. Even its eyelids had protective plates!

Ankylosaurus

Both *Ankylosaurus* and *Stegosaurus* had unique tails. While *Stegosaurus* had spikes at the end of its tail, *Ankylosaurus* had a cluster of bones forming a club. One swing of its tail and *Ankylosaurus* could shatter the bones of its predators!

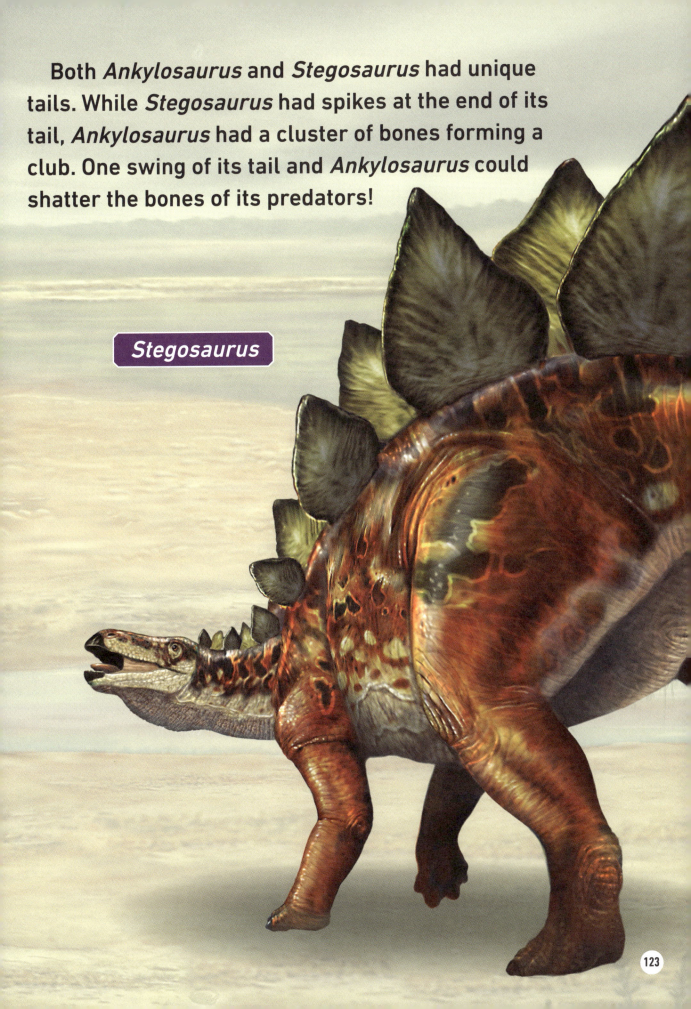

Stegosaurus

FUELED BY PLANTS

Flowers and plants grew more diverse during the Cretaceous period. The first flowering plants emerged at this time. This truck-sized dinosaur needed fuel, and it had to eat a lot of plants to keep its energy up.

Ankylosaurus walked close to the ground on its short legs, grazing on low-lying plants. It snipped off plant pieces with its sharp beak and small teeth. But it didn't chew them! *Ankylosaurus* swallowed each bite whole. The bacteria in its stomach helped break down the plant food.

JOIN THE CLUB

With its heavy armor and slow speed, *Ankylosaurus* likely lived alone. However, *Ankylosaurus* fossils have been uncovered in mass death assemblages in the United States, Hungary, and Mongolia. Mass death assemblages are fossil sites with a large amount of dinosaur bones from the same time period.

These groups of fossils demonstrated that some *Ankylosaurus* lived in herds. Scientists now believe that *Ankylosaurus* may have lived in herds at only certain times during their lives.

ZUUL THE COMPETITOR

In 2014, one ankylosaur called *Zuul crurivastator* was discovered in the Judith River Formation in the United States. Its well-preserved skin, head, tail, and bony armor revealed an interesting trait. Zuul had a blunt-shaped injury around its hip. If it had been attacked by a predator, Zuul would have had more varied injuries on its body. But this isolated injury was shaped like a club . . . Zuul was hit by another ankylosaur!

This discovery suggested that the clubbed tail was used for more than just protection from predators. *Ankylosaurus* used its tail to strike others of its kind to compete for resources and territory.

Zuul's fossil

ARMORED ANKYLOSAURUS

Ankylosaurus was as big as a tank and was protected like one too. It roamed its habitat slowly, swallowing plants along the way. If a predator did come close, *Ankylosaurus* swung its long tail and struck the predator. The discovery of and new research into *Ankylosaurus* fossils continue to reveal more about this heavily armored dinosaur.

Prehistoric Animals in the Air and in the Sea

By Devra Newberger Speregen

In a part of North America that will one day become Texas, *Tyrannosaurus rex* (tie-RAN-oh-SORE-us rex) tears into his morning meal—a dead dinosaur he found by the marsh. *T. rex* is the biggest, most ferocious predator of the Late Cretaceous period. He is so large and so fearsome that when other dinosaurs hear him stomping nearby, many run for their lives!

With his supersharp eyesight, *Quetzalcoatlus* (KWET-zal-koh-AT-lus) sees *T. rex* from above. *Quetzalcoatlus* is not a dinosaur. He is a pterosaur, or a flying reptile. Like other pterosaurs, *Quetzalcoatlus* has wings and can fly.

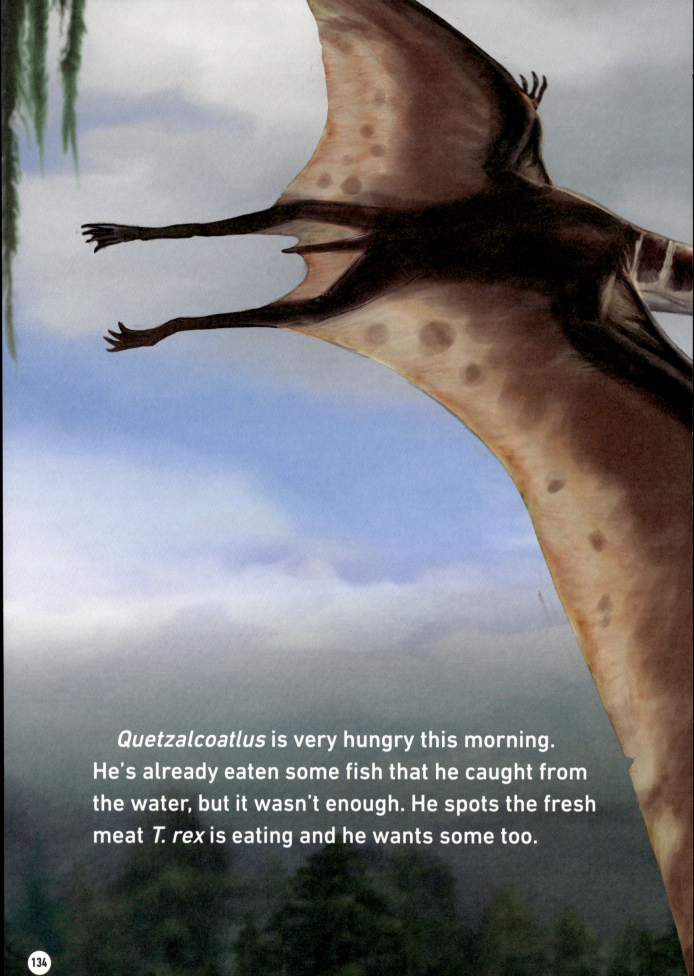

Quetzalcoatlus is very hungry this morning. He's already eaten some fish that he caught from the water, but it wasn't enough. He spots the fresh meat *T. rex* is eating and he wants some too.

Quetzalcoatlus weighs about 500 pounds and has a 40-foot wingspan. He is the largest pterosaur of all time. Still, he's no match for *T. rex,* who weighs 15,000 pounds and has a bone-crushing bite. But *Quetzalcoatlus* is strong. And though he doesn't have teeth, he has a powerful beak. And he has something *T. rex* does not have: the ability to fly!

Flying gives *Quetzalcoatlus* an edge over *T. rex*. He can swoop down and surprise the mighty dinosaur from above. And he can hover over *T. rex* to attack the top of his head with his 6-foot-long beak.

If he gets lucky, *Quetzalcoatlus* can attack him in the eyes too. Without sight, *T. rex* won't be able to find food and will surely die.

Quetzalcoatlus descends while keeping a close watch on *T. rex*. *T. rex* is so distracted by the delicious meal that he doesn't see *Quetzalcoatlus* flying closer. *Quetzalcoatlus* goes right for *T. rex*'s head, stabbing at the dinosaur with his long, strong beak and sharp toe claws! *T. rex* retreats; he is no match for *Quetzalcoatlus*'s gargantuan wings and dominating attack from the air.

Quetzalcoatlus digs his beak deep into the animal flesh. *T. rex*'s sharp teeth have already done all the hard work for him. Now *Quetzalcoatlus* can rip the meat into smaller pieces he can swallow. He eats quickly, watching out for *T. rex*'s return.

But there's a sound nearby; a new *T. rex* has sniffed out the meal! *Quetzalcoatlus* needs to fly away, and fast! *Quetzalcoatlus* takes a "jumping start." He pushes off of his powerful back legs and jumps 8 feet into the air. Then he flaps his massive wings . . . just in time to escape!

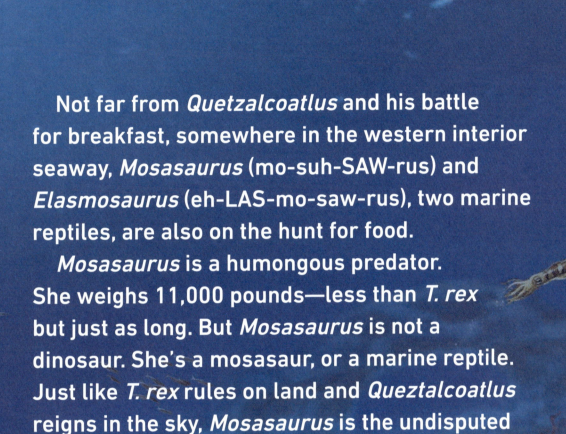

Not far from *Quetzalcoatlus* and his battle for breakfast, somewhere in the western interior seaway, *Mosasaurus* (mo-suh-SAW-rus) and *Elasmosaurus* (eh-LAS-mo-saw-rus), two marine reptiles, are also on the hunt for food.

Mosasaurus is a humongous predator. She weighs 11,000 pounds—less than *T. rex* but just as long. But *Mosasaurus* is not a dinosaur. She's a mosasaur, or a marine reptile. Just like *T. rex* rules on land and *Queztalcoatlus* reigns in the sky, *Mosasaurus* is the undisputed queen of the seas!

As she does every morning, *Mosasaurus* surveys her underwater habitat, searching for prey. A sea turtle, big fish, or even another mosasaur would be the perfect morning meal for *Mosasaurus*. But first, she needs to take a break from hunting. As an air breather, *Mosasaurus* needs to surface to breathe air.

Elasmosaurus, a huge plesiosaur, or long-necked marine reptile, lives in the same waterway as *Mosasaurus*. He is also hunting for food this morning. He's been trailing after a fish, using his flippers to propel him through the water. But when he closes in on his prey, he spots something enormous hovering near the surface.

It's *Mosasaurus*! The mosasaur is much bigger and stronger than he is and is known to eat plesiosaurs like him. *Elasmosaurus* must get to the fish before *Mosasaurus* does. Luckily, *Elasmosaurus* has an advantage over *Mosasaurus*: a 23-foot-long neck that allows it to take prey by surprise.

Though *Elasmosaurus* has the advantage of a long neck allowing it to sneak up on schools of fish, this aquatic creature isn't as fast as *Mosasaurus*. *Elasmosaurus* must go into action—quick—before *Mosasaurus* submerges again.

Elasmosaurus can't make any mistakes. If the mosasaur catches him, she will tear him apart. But this is where having a long neck comes in handy. *Elasmosaurus* swoops in, opens his mighty jaws, and sinks his sharp teeth into the fish. At the same time, *Mosasaurus* has been distracted by a meal near the water's surface. *Elasmosaurus* has escaped danger and come out of it with a meal!

A CLOSER LOOK: *TRICERATOPS*

By Dienesa Le

147

TRICERATOPS TIME

During the Late Cretaceous period, *Triceratops* (tri-SER-ah-tops) roamed what is now western North America. *Triceratops* belonged to a diverse group of dinosaurs called ornithischians, or bird-hipped dinosaurs. Specifically, *Triceratops* was a ceratopsian, a horned dinosaur.

Triceratops was one of the more dominant herbivores and lived until the mass extinction 66 million years ago that killed the non-bird dinosaurs and many other plants and animals. *Triceratops* had three horns and a large frill to protect itself against predators, including one of the fiercest of its time . . . *T. rex*.

TRICERATOPS UP CLOSE

STATS
PRONUNCIATION: **tri-SER-ah-tops**
NAME MEANING: **Three-Horned Face**
SIZE: **Up to 30 feet long; Over 18,000 pounds**
WHEN IT LIVED: **Cretaceous**
FOSSILS FOUND: **North America**

This large dinosaur supported its weight on four short legs. Each leg had hooflike fingers.

A STRONG SHIELD

One of the most recognizable dinosaurs, *Triceratops* is known for the bony frill around its neck. This frill grew up to 4 feet across and guarded its body like a shield. However, *Triceratops* did not always succeed in protecting itself. Some *Triceratops* fossils have puncture marks on the frills from dueling other *Triceratops*.

But the frill was helpful in other ways. It contained blood vessels that might have flashed bright colors to attract mates or send warnings. The frill may have identified *Triceratops* from others in its herd.

THREE HORNS

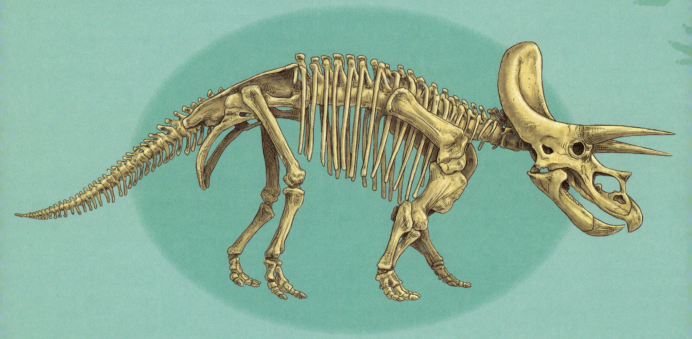

While the frill was a shield of protection, *Triceratops* had three horns to use as weapons for defense. The two long horns on its brow were sharp enough to strike through predators and to fight other *Triceratops* for mates. The third horn on its snout was shorter, but still useful for defense.

All three horns were made of bone covered by a sheath of keratin—just like cow horns today. Keratin is the same material that makes up human fingernails.

HUNDREDS OF TEETH

As a herbivore, *Triceratops*'s parrotlike beak was perfect for grasping plants, and 144 to 160 teeth at the back of its mouth broke the plants down. Each tooth had five layers of tissue. As *Triceratops* chewed, the teeth wore down and became knifelike.

The sharpened teeth could slice and break up tough forest plants. *Triceratops* shed and replaced hundreds of these incredible teeth throughout its lifetime.

DINOSAUR RELATIVES

Protoceratops (pro-toe-SER-ah-tops) was an early relative of *Triceratops*. Like *Triceratops*, *Protoceratops* walked on all four legs, but its shorter front legs created an arch in its back. *Protoceratops* had a small frill like *Triceratops*, but did not have any horns.

Protoceratops

Centrosaurus

Another close relative, *Centrosaurus* (cen-troh-SORE-us), had a frill too. But unlike *Triceratops*, *Centrosaurus*'s frill was too thin to protect it very well. It used its frill to attract mates or distinguish itself in a herd.

BONE WARS

During the 1800s, two paleontologists, Othniel Charles Marsh and Edward Drinker Cope, competed in a heated fossil race called the bone wars. They wanted to see who could discover the most dinosaurs in the United States. Their crews spied on each other and even stole their rival's fossils!

Othniel Charles Marsh

Edward Drinker Cope

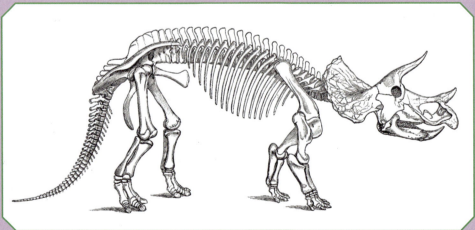

In 1887, George Lyman Cannon discovered a partial skull fossil of a *Triceratops* and sent it to Marsh. Marsh originally thought it belonged to a bison. But when he saw another similar fossil, Marsh realized they both were from a horned dinosaur species. He called this dinosaur *Triceratops* after the three horns on its head.

LEARNING FROM FOSSILS

Triceratops fossils are one of the most discovered dinosaur fossils today. Specifically, large skull fossils featuring the distinct frill and horns have been uncovered. These fascinating fossils provide clues into the life of this prehistoric giant.

Velociraptor versus Protoceratops

By Courtney Acampora

The sun rises over the desert, casting the sand dunes in a golden glow. The rising sun means it's time for breakfast for *Velociraptor* (vel-OSS-ee-RAP-tor).

At only 6 feet long and 35 pounds, this meat eater is small but mighty. His name means "fast thief" because in addition to hunting his meals, he will steal them too.

Nearby, *Velociraptor* hears footsteps. It's his fellow *Velociraptors* who have also woken up and are ready for a meal. With fast feet that can run up to 24 miles an hour, these speedy predators are able to capture most meals that they come across.

What's on the menu today? *Velociraptors* love snacking on small mammals, lizards, eggs . . . and even baby *Velociraptors*. Luckily, with excellent senses such as smell and eyesight, this *Velociraptor* won't have a problem finding a meal.

Velociraptor is covered in feathers, but it can't fly. As a male *Velociraptor*, this dinosaur sports brightly colored feathers that are sure to attract a mate. He's bipedal, meaning he moves on two legs, using his long tail for balance. These swift movements help *Velociraptor* chase down his prey.

Now it's time to eat. He has speed and 4-inch retractable, razor-sharp claws that he'll use to latch onto prey without a problem. What's that smell? *Velociraptor* runs toward the scent—it smells like breakfast.

Near a sand dune, *Velociraptor* spots *Protoceratops* (pro-toe-SER-ah-tops), a small plant eater the size of a sheep, and a relative of *Triceratops* (tri-SER-ah-tops). At only 2-feet tall and 200 pounds, *Protoceratops* uses its sharp beak to snip off leaves to eat and to defend itself from predators . . . like *Velociraptor*.

Protoceratops lives in a herd, where there is safety in numbers. However, this *Protoceratops* spotted a plant that was too good to resist. He has wandered away from his herd for this delectable breakfast. And now he's vulnerable and on display for predators.

Velociraptor digs his sharp-clawed feet into the sand and he's off, racing toward *Protoceratops*. *Protoceratops* turns his frill-covered head and sees *Velociraptor* sprinting toward him. *Protoceratops*'s barrel-shaped body is not meant for speed, but he runs off to the best of his ability.

Despite his attempt at running, *Protoceratops* is slow-moving. He can't keep up with *Velociraptor*'s speed and agility. *Velociraptor* is close—close enough to stab his sickle claw into *Protoceratops*'s neck.

Crash! Protoceratops and *Velociraptor* tumble to the ground. *Protoceratops* has a strong jaw and beak and he's ready to use them. He chomps down on *Velociraptor*'s arm. *Velociraptor* screeches in pain as the two dinosaurs wrestle.

Both dinosaurs suffer major blows. *Protoceratops* writhes in pain as *Velociraptor*'s sickle claw latches onto his neck. *Velociraptor* kicks and strikes *Protoceratops*'s belly. While *Protoceratops*'s beak is useful for plucking leaves, it's so strong that it has broken *Velociraptor*'s arm.

Nearby, other *Protoceratops* watch the scuffle between *Protoceratops* and *Velociraptor* and count themselves lucky that they weren't the chosen victim. But equally as distracting are the strong winds that have started kicking up the sand.

In this dry and dusty landscape, sandstorms are a regular occurrence. The herd of *Protoceratops* starts moving away from the sandstorm's path. But the *Protoceratops* and *Velociraptor* continue to fight, unfazed by the sudden weather change.

Locked in their fierce battle, *Protoceratops* and *Velociraptor* continue their fight. *Velociraptor* is determined to defeat *Protoceratops* so he can have a hearty meal. *Protoceratops* uses all the strength he can muster to escape and survive *Velociraptor*'s deadly fight. Meanwhile, the sandstorm has strengthened and caused a sand dune to collapse onto the fighting pair!

The sand from the nearby dune has buried the fighting dinosaurs. The weight of the sand makes the two dinosaurs' escape impossible. They will die in the sand, forever frozen in combat. Millions of years later, humans will discover the fossil of these two dinosaurs in battle—a snapshot of a fight that has survived millions of years.

A CLOSER LOOK: *SPINOSAURUS*

By Devra Newberger Speregen

MEET SPINOSAURUS

Spinosaurus (SPINE-oh-SORE-us) roamed the earth about 100 million years ago during the Late Cretaceous period. Its name means "spiny reptile," because of the 6-foot-tall spines on its back. The spines stuck up and formed an arch that looked like a sailboat's sail.

SPINOSAURUS UP CLOSE

Spinosaurus had a narrow snout like a crocodile's with nostrils closer to the eyes, which allowed for the snout to be submerged in water to catch fish.

Spinosaurus had a long, arched sail made up of 6- to 7-foot-long spines that stood tall on its back. The sail may have been used to attract mates.

Spinosaurus's sharp teeth were smooth, straight, and cone-shaped, ideal for catching fish. It continuously replaced its teeth throughout its life.

Spinosaurus had strong jaws for feeding on fish. Its teeth were tilted to keep fish inside its mouth.

STATS
PRONUNCIATION: **SPINE-oh-SORE-us**
NAME MEANING: **Spiny Reptile**
SIZE: **52 feet long; 16,000 pounds**
WHEN IT LIVED: **Late Cretaceous**
FOSSILS FOUND: **Northern Africa (Egypt and Morocco)**

Spinosaurus's tail had tall, thin spines like on its sail.

Spinosaurus had dense bones. Scientists are not quite sure why yet.

SPINOSAURUS DISCOVERY

In 1911, a German paleontologist named Ernst Stromer was on an expedition in Egypt, searching for dinosaur fossils. While digging at Bahariya Oasis, he uncovered a partial dinosaur skeleton. He carefully removed the dinosaur teeth and bones and shipped them home to Germany to study more closely.

Stromer didn't have enough bones to piece together a full skeleton, but he had enough to know he'd discovered a new dinosaur. Stromer called this new dinosaur *Spinosaurus*.

Bahariya Oasis

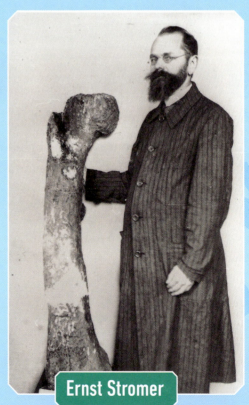
Ernst Stromer

Here are some of the *Spinosaurus* bones, teeth, and fossils Ernst Stromer found embedded in a 95-million-year-old layer of rock in Egypt:

- Lower jawbone
- Some crocodile-like teeth
- Backbones, each with a 6-foot-tall spine
- 37-inch femur (thigh bone)
- 3½-foot-long, 5-inch-thick upper extremity bone

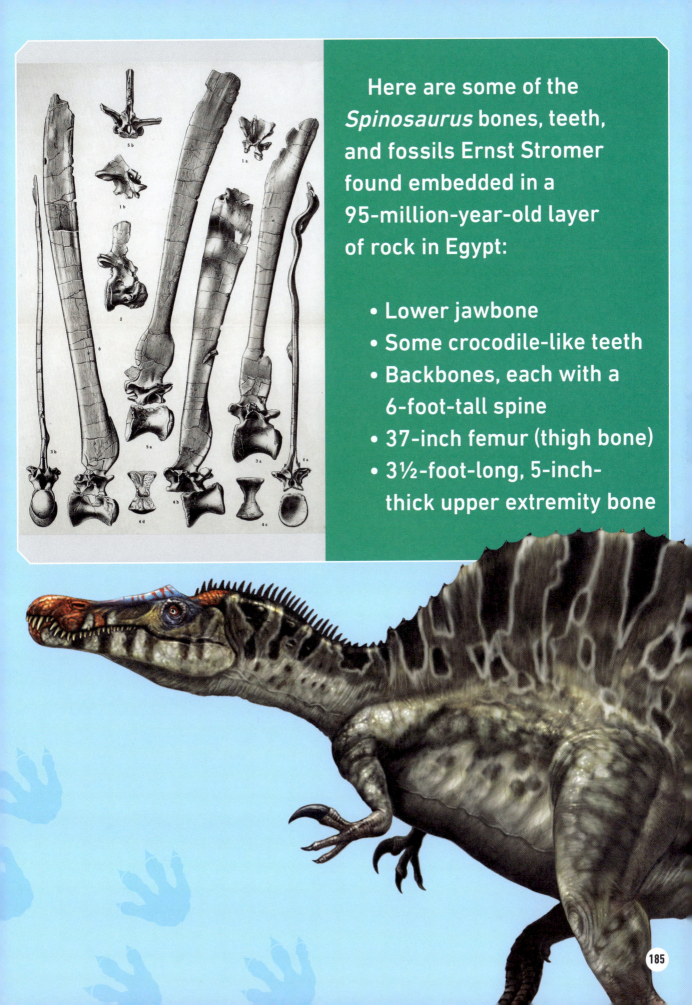

ONE PUZZLING DINOSAUR

For paleontologists, dinosaur skeletons are like puzzles. First, they must figure out which bones were connected. The more bones, the better understanding of the dinosaur's form. But for Stromer, the bones he found sparked many questions. Did *Spinosaurus* walk on two legs or four? Did *Spinosaurus* live on land or in water?

Luckily, paleontologists continued to search for *Spinosaurus* fossils. They found more fossils in Algeria in the 1970s and 1990s. And in 2011 and 2014, paleontologist Nizar Ibrahim discovered another, more complete *Spinosaurus* skeleton in Morocco.

Spinosaurus Jawbone

AN EVER-CHANGING SKELETON

Details about *Spinosaurus* have changed so many times in the 100 years since its discovery that scientists are still scratching their heads, trying to figure out more about this dinosaur species.

What Still Baffles Scientists About *Spinosaurus*?

- Did *Spinosaurus* walk on two legs or four legs?
- Did *Spinosaurus* live on land or in water?
- What was *Spinosaurus*'s sail used for?

In 2023, paleontologist Paul Sereno believed that with such a huge body and sail, *Spinosaurus* would have been a terrible swimmer and unable to survive underwater.

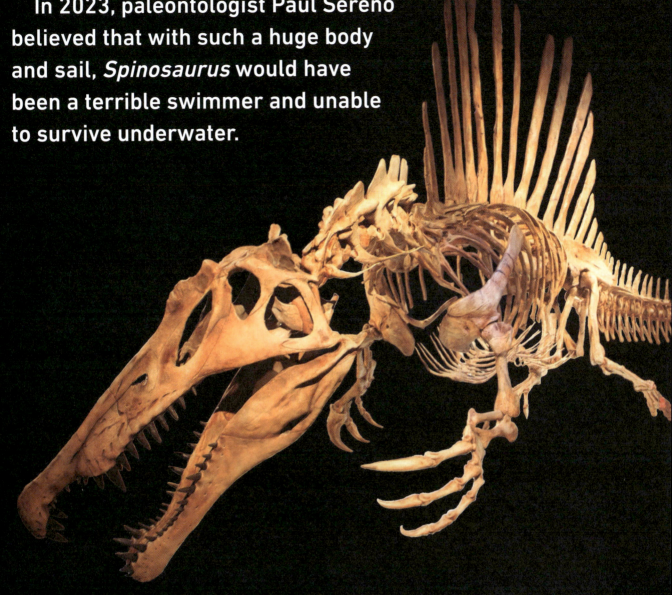

Spinosaurus Vertebrae

WHAT DO YOU THINK?

Here are some facts about *Spinosaurus*. What does each fact tell you about the type of dinosaur *Spinosaurus* was?

The area in North Africa where *Spinosaurus* remains have been found was wet, swampy, and marshy 95 million years ago.
Maybe *Spinosaurus* lived in water.

Spinosaurus specimens have been found with wide tails like an alligator's that might have helped propel them in the water.
Maybe *Spinosaurus* lived in water.

Spinosaurus had nostrils far back on its snout where it could keep them out of the water.
Maybe *Spinosaurus* lived in water.

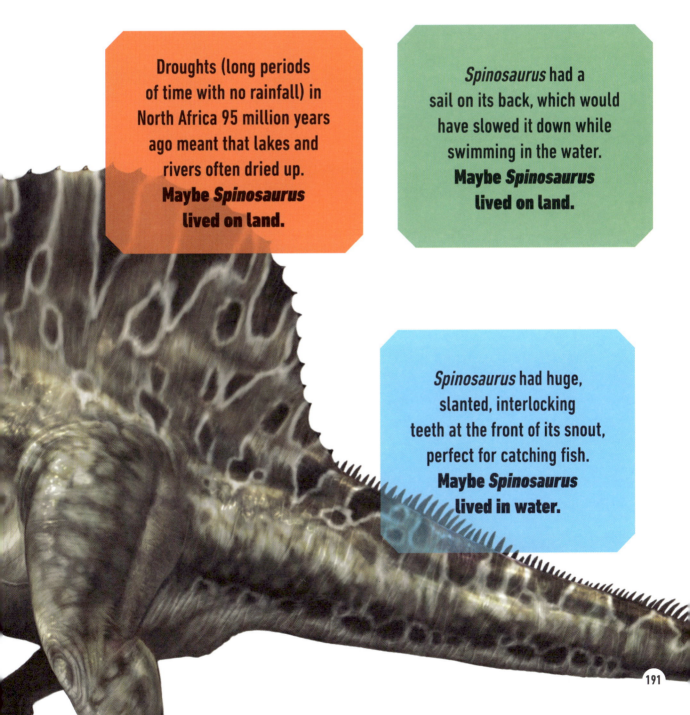

Spinosaurus's clawed hands would not have been good at paddling and swimming. **Maybe *Spinosaurus* didn't use those hands to swim but lived on land.**

With its heavy, 50-foot-long body, *Spinosaurus* likely couldn't get around easily underwater. **Maybe *Spinosaurus* lived on land.**

Droughts (long periods of time with no rainfall) in North Africa 95 million years ago meant that lakes and rivers often dried up. **Maybe *Spinosaurus* lived on land.**

Spinosaurus had a sail on its back, which would have slowed it down while swimming in the water. **Maybe *Spinosaurus* lived on land.**

Spinosaurus had huge, slanted, interlocking teeth at the front of its snout, perfect for catching fish. **Maybe *Spinosaurus* lived in water.**

191

LAND OR SEA?

When it comes to all the guessing about *Spinosaurus*... who's right? There's evidence to suggest it lived on land and in water. And while a swimming theropod dinosaur goes against everything paleontologists have learned about land dinosaurs until now, maybe *Spinosaurus* just happens to be the first!